North of Zenith

poems by

Lindy Obach

Finishing Line Press
Georgetown, Kentucky

North of Zenith

ACKNOWLEDGMENTS

2015 *Scurfpea Anthology: The Scandalous Lives of Butterflies*: "The ABCs of Love,"
"Leather Stretcher"
2014 SDS Poetry Society's *Pasque Petals*: "How a Midwest Farm Girl Tells You She
    Loves You"
2014 *Scurfpea Anthology: Memory, Echo, Words*: "Unsettled," "bunkhouse"
Fall 2014 *South Dakota Women: Action, Influence, and Voice*: "Rowboat"
Vol. 50 (2013), *South Dakota Review*: "Paraska in Spring"
Issue 9 (Spring 2013) of *Midwestern Gothic*: "In Case I Croak"
January 2013 Issue of *(605) Magazine*: "What Reminds Us of a Beating Heart,"
    "Southwest by Dakota," "Haircuts on the Back Porch"
Issue 1.4 (Summer 2012) of *The Blue Bear Review*: "On the Wind that Won't Quit,
    Just Before 8 o'clock," "The Old Red Trail," "The Boot Falls Heavy"
Fall 2011 *Ukrainian Cultural Institute*: "Her Sunday"
Volume 48.4 (2012), *South Dakota Review*: "What the Missouri River Will Tell You, If
    You Let It"
2007 *Vermillion Literary Project* Magazine: "My Dear,"

Publisher: Leah Maines

Editor: Christen Kincaid

Cover Art: Meriah Jacobs-Frost, www.facebook.com/DancingLotusMama

Author Photo: Lindy Obach

Cover Design: Elizabeth Maines

Printed in the USA on acid-free paper.
Order online: www.finishinglinepress.com
        also available on amazon.com

Author inquiries and mail orders:
Finishing Line Press
P. O. Box 1626
Georgetown, Kentucky 40324
U. S. A.

Table of Contents

"Oh give me land, lots of land
under starry skies above.
Don't fence me in."
Cole Porter and Robert Fletcher

Zenith, ND was established in 1903 and the population hit its peak of about 80 in the 1920s. At Zenith's biggest, it had a school, a post office, a grain elevator, a bar, and coal mines. In 1940 the population dropped to about 20 people, and the town disappeared from maps in the 1960s. My family farm, established in 1908, is about two miles north of where Zenith used to exist.

Unsettled

I come from a long line
of dead people.
—from "Bones" by Libby Roderick

What do we unearth?

We kick up shards of pottery,
thick-glassed bottle bottoms, smoothed
by the prairie wind. We dig out browned
medicine flasks and thumb away gray dirt.
We look for ourselves through the
caving doorways and sagging, empty windows
of an old pine-planked farmhouse, a kit home
from Montgomery Ward.
We squint to see the great-grandmother,
gone now for half a century, spooning syrup
down a raw throat in her snug kitchen.

To walk down a gravel road,
to spread our arms wide on each side,
to spin in circles as the fixed origin of budding wheat, barley, and
oat.
To wonder what this summer fallow looked like before:
Rising butte, sloping riverbank, clumped pasture.
Wild. Heaving with life.

My father walks the ditches
and wrests leafy spurge from the wild roses.
We plant cottonwoods and golden willows while
a red-tailed hawk bulked on a fence post
watches; her neck
hunches against the biting wind.

Our hearts swell when we bend to uproot these
little pieces of what used to be;
when a flint arrowhead pokes through the soil,
when the stone foundation of the century-old
Zenith post office still stands low,
when we look down at the hands folded in our laps
and see they are our mother's.

What is buried
(was buried)
crests toward us,
over and over and over.

Harvest

For Shawn, 1985 - 2002

North Dakota summers used
to be enough to bring you back.

Bleached-flour hair, lashes so long.
A sixteenth of Creek in your blood
and a Tulsa accent.
Skinny legs like stalks of wild oats
spreading through crisp wheat fields.

You'd last maybe one round in the combine.
I'd watch from a scoria approach for you to
jump down from the Gleaner and high-step
your way back to me, knobby knees
welted from fresh-cut grain.

I miss the mole at the corner of your mouth—
how it made your face look
smudged and dirty,
and young.

On the way to your funeral,
an exit somewhere in Kansas promised
honey and sweet water.

I've been reaching out to
every skinny seventeen year old
I see.
I'm just as protective as their mothers,
if some strange woman grabbed their sons
and shook.
My hands have been knocked
away so much
my knuckles are bruised.

We stopped farming this year.
For the first time in so many years,
we won't have a crop.

I wonder if
grayed-out section lines,
blowing chaff,
fallowed squares of soil,
will remind me of you.

Garlic Avenue

Everyone in town calls this tiny plane of blacktop
Garlic Avenue
because Ukrainians
used to line this narrow, broken street,
and the smells from mothers' kitchens
of onions, cream, sausage, and garlic
hung thick in our ponytails and corduroys.

When we were sixteen, the boy I was in love with
drove Garlic Avenue with me next to him,
and we were hungry.

We were always hungry and searching.
We could not believe that this crumbling
Main Street was our town, this weed-ridden football field
our Friday nights,
this 1972 Ford Galaxie our escape.

Now Garlic Avenue sits empty with its kitchens
boarded up, and we can't remember any
Ukrainian, not even the New Year blessing, not even the swear
words we used to sling back and forth so well.
We miss the singing:
"Oh give me a dime, for dance and for show,
and I'll think of you, honey, wherever I go."
And so much we miss the food!
The pyrohy and the braided bread,
the eating on sopping paper plates while a violin and dulcimer
play a Hopak to velveteen shoulders pressed against each other,
heels turning,
singing in between pulls of champagne and homemade red-eye.
To stomping red boots and dark wrists canted over
one another's shoulders, linked and threaded, like the ribbons,
blue (sky) and yellow (wheatfields)
sluicing down
our dancing backs.

The ABCs of Love

Any idiot can see I am in love with you
because: your hair is my lifeboat; beneath your
chestbone beats the most lovely organ
da-dum, da-dum, da-dum
every second I lay my ear to your heated skin. A
frenzied *Hallelujah!* breaks out in my head,
growing more green and beautiful each day.
Hollyhocks shoot up through my veins, and
I want to root myself wherever you are, always.
January mornings with you were divine; the wind
knifed around our too-tall house while, inside,
Love bloomed.
Maybe we are envied. Or, maybe
no one cares.
Only this is what matters: the time you
prayed over my burst appendix. The time you
quilted my life to yours. The time you
ran my burnt fingers under the cool
stream of the kitchen faucet.
Take my hand.
Underneath my jacket, palm my heart.
VFW line dance with me.
Weight your body to mine, but be careful of my
xiphoid process.
Yoke yourself to me so I can
zero in on your traceable freckles.

bunkhouse

my dad showed up back at the farm
after four Navy years spent on the USS Floyd B. Parks
      circumnavigating the Japanese Islands
            a greenish-gray eagle inked into his left bicep

but he didn't live in the house with his Mother
her the reason he lied in the first place
and said he was eighteen just to get away
      away from the prairie the cattle the Slavic beatings

she was of the Old Country
where fists and vodka were slugged with equal abandon
      her house tired and drafty
            veiled deep within an acreage of ponderosa pines

instead he lived in the bunkhouse
a primer-soaked hut so old
      the despondent glass of the window panes had slid downward
            time has since made the filmy slabs fatter at the sill

my dad woke one biting cold night
to mice chewing on his eyebrows
      they were hungry for the salt
         work left on his skin

he stayed and worked that loamy
Steppe-like land until it grew green
      he raised us alongside barley and vowed
         to never again let another creature get the best of him

later the descendants of those self-assured mice
ran us out of our first trailer house
      the one we sold to a family
         poorer and colder than us

The Old Red Trail

Mid-December: I am on my way home
slicing through cornfields that give way
to sugarbeets that give way to pasture

mapped with the criss-cross of cattle trails.
My used Ford is packed with three semesters
of grad school, overstuffed like the cannoli

I ate at the State Fair last summer that tasted
like deep-fryer and somehow, New York City to me,
though I've never been.

The drive is like a 36 inch inseam, and as
predictable as canned beer on a Friday night.
I scan the horizon for something amazing:

a pack of leathered bikers with frozen beards,
a plaid-hatted farmer doing a controlled
burn that is, suddenly, uncontrollable.

It's quiet. Still as well water.
I ache for anything loud,
but as tenderized as this stretch of I-29 is,

the radio crackles and hisses and proselytizes at me.
When the numbers finally stop on a clear channel,
Paul Harvey

isn't sweet, and he doesn't remind me of the farm.
Today, his old voice talks of a pregnant woman
found murdered and childless, of

a Philadelphia orchestra conductor who threw
himself out of a window. Almost,
I begin to cry.

It's winter. The land at the Dakota border
is wind beaten and bone dry.
Nobody is talking snow.

Southwest by Dakota

Because you have now promised
to take me
to your red Southwest, I want to
promise you the same.

Let me take you
to my Southwest,
broken by Badlands and shadowed
by sagebrush.
We could walk the trails I built
and carve names, sweet nothings
into the sandstone walls
of Maah Daah Hey
switchbacks.
Mindful of water bars,
I will lead you,
eyes closed,
deep into scoria hills,
burning coal veins, my
summer.

Because your braid is thick,
long, dark enough,
would you let me use your rope
to tether my raft
after we wind through shallow
river branches along
the old-man stubble of
spring wheat?

The pine shelter belt has grown tall
enough now,
taller than how I feel
laying next
to you on a twin-bed.

A row of Chokecherry trees,
sticky like jam,
leaves thin scratches on my wrists
when I untangle myself
from the thought of you.

I dream of your Southwest:
What sun-spotted lizards
will you place in my weak-hearted
palm? Will you halt me with a
hand to my thigh to show me blooming
Desert Chicory?

My Southwest can
sting like brine,
goes down easy and smooth
only for locals.

Come.
Drink with me.
Tip your head back and
let me gently stroke your
white throat.

What Reminds Us of a Beating Heart

The penne slips
from the boiling pot
into the blue colander
one of us bought before
we even knew the other existed,
and I think of those
tiny silver fish
swimming tight
together, moving as one,
crimson-tipped gills
slick, eyes bulbous
and flashing.

On the Wind That Won't Quit, Just Before 8 o'clock

I am windburned.
My skin radiates, would melt you
like a pair of popsicles slipped into
a hot mouth.

The wind:
today, yesterday, tomorrow,
knocks garbage cans into the street;
yellow finches sway with the buoyant feeder,
maple seeds spin like downed helicopters.

Tonight, wind
will wake me, will remind me
of a single-wide in the middle
of the prairie, of running across
an open yard in the darkest part
of the night to the safety of a
concrete basement.

I wish I had this picture:
me, no more than six,
posed in my mother's
pom pom girl outfit.
Royal purple.
My haystack hair is
bleached at the top, split
ends from the everyday wind.
Brown legs poking out
from the pleated skirt,
crooked teeth.
It is summer, and I
am silly.

The wind:
now,
won't quit.
Of all the things that drove my
father out of the flatlands,
the stinging, the howling,
should have been
that last straw.

Give me time,

for
I am still clinging
like peached syrup
to this hope
that one day
I will walk up the front stoop
and open
the cherry red door
to find you painting
our kitchen walls.
We will smile quietly
at each other.
I will then head to the back shed
to prime the mower
and cut grass
until you call me in for
a dinner of cold sandwiches
and salted tomatoes
fresh from the garden.

My Life as Hair

I.

I am eight. By some act of God, my mother lets me choose my hairstyle. Since I am more boy than most of the jug-headed boys in my class, I opt for long in the back with a spike on top. My sides are shaped into soft points, the top of my head is thick, lush, brown spikes. A little on the longish side. The back is straight and hangs down past my shoulders. I can't stop looking at myself in the mirror. After I get the haircut, we go to the mall and I am the coolest kid in Kmart. I go to the arcade with my brother, and he's embarrassed by me but likes when I watch him play Mortal Kombat and cheer him on. "Watch me rip this guy's spine out, Lu." I want to be just like him. I beg my mom to let me take my shirt off on sticky July afternoons and run around the farm like the boys. I tip over the garbage can in my brother's bathroom, trying to pee standing up. I have this ache.

II.

I am fifteen. My hair is often in a ponytail because I am one of the starting five on the JV basketball team and we do nothing but win all year long. My hair is thick, honeyed, and long, shaggy bangs hang in my eyes. My hormones are in overdrive. That year, I will finally give up and grow out my bangs. Instantly, I am better-looking and, for the first time, have hair my friends can't stop touching. "Jennifer Aniston hair!" they all squeal when I walk to my locker that morning at school. I spend the rest of the year in the back of the neighbor boy's LTD, which is mostly fun. I look at some of my friends from other schools and think, *if I were a boy, I'd totally date her.* Then, I blush. My shoulders and neck redden, and I shake my head to blur and to soften the edges of these thoughts.

III.

I am twenty-two. I've got mostly good hair now; it's soft and layered and parted just like *Glamour* commands, but since I've always liked big, big hair, it just emphasizes my fat face. Still, I spend a lot of time on my hair—I like this girl and want to look good for her. Our first apartment together is a hovel on top of a rickety house and our long strands of hair drape the slant-roofed bathroom. No one knows about this girl, and the amount of backpedaling I do to keep it this way is exhausting, and sometimes, my guard falls. One of these times, a dark-haired professor spots the opening and draws blood. I am wounded.

IV.

I am thirty-three. I have another degree and I teach. Writing mostly, but really, competency. I secretly hope that one of my students will comment on my evals, "she's a good teacher, but her hair is awesome." Now, my hair is held back with a bandana because I am painting the fence on the house we just bought, or it is short because my girl loves running her hands up my corded neck, or I am tucking a loose, silvery strand behind my ear as I transplant purple bearded irises. I don't take credit for my hair anymore—*it's from my mom*, I say. *She's got a mop of thick, stick-straight hair, and I am only lucky that I got it.*

My Dear,

Hanging pictures your sister painted for us up in the new kitchen.
It's almost complete now, and Bobby Darin sings
in the background, smooth voice warms
through the scratches of the needle.
(Because I want a girl to call my own.)
It's a balmy night, almost.
I watched you all evening, thinking of this new life
we might get to have.
Rooms full of books and music
and it's almost complete now.

I went out and bought plants tonight; I couldn't help it.
From the unraked backyard, I can see into our kitchen,
and I can tell it's a good kitchen.
Soft glow, glass bottles, a wine rack half full.
Walls painted to look like a northern sunset, streaky gold
and warm to the touch.
An entire cupboard dedicated to baking.
The refrigerator is stuck full of pictures
and postcards and magnets.
We love and are loved.
I wrote silly things on the grocery list
and waited until you noticed and laughed.

Close to midnight. I step outside.
The brick leading to the front door
is being thrust up by earth and moss,
but I do not want to fix it.
It feels a little wild, a little untamed, beneath my shoes.
Will the tulips come up in the Spring?
I'm afraid I did not plant them deep enough.
The way you brush my face as you pass
may be enough to coax the bulbs into long slivers
of green leaf and bright vases of red, of purple, of deep blue.

It's late. Come give me your hand, the night is warm.

Though I am ready for the first night and the first snow,
I would like to press my lips to the white hollow
of your wrist and think that I still taste summer.

The Boot Falls Heavy

I.
The boot falls heavy on a slice of metal,
the earth gives easy,
and a tanned wrist hauls another shovelful away.

II.
Once, this is all they had.
Muscles, tendons, knuckles.
The sweat-smoothed wood of
rakes, shovels, pitchforks, an axe.
Hay fever, clogged ducts, shafts of light
falling onto the warped floorboards.
He thought about what was ahead –
broken ribs, pain and blood and promises and sighs.
Daybreak and hail. Birth. Concrete and chicken coops
and raw, tender hearts.
He thought about her. He thought about his grandchildren,
a spark decades away, so faint it was almost invisible.
He thought he would put up a basketball hoop; someone, maybe sometime,
might like to play a game of Pig.

III.
He had a way of standing. Always in profile, hands on hips, face
down-tilted toward the scoria ground.
Shadows cast onto the orange-pink shards, long and lean.
Squinting, he looked into her face, and she rubbed the
raised veins on the back of his forearm, the calloused web of his hand.
She had a way of smiling soft.

IV.
He did this all for her.

V.
They liked evening best. Mourning doves
called from across the dimming yard, persistent and plaintive,
the sinking sun glinting
off the dusty panes of the barn, waning and hopeful.
Meatloaf in the oven.

A spark flares quick,
(almost imperceptible)
interrupts the quiet air.

What The Missouri River Will Tell You, If You Let It

The sky:
blue,
blank,
yellow,
purple.
Then,
        river.

A Canada goose, alone
in the middle of this span
of water, will call out until hoarse,
until her big-winged mate returns.

My fear of heights is softened
by the banks of duned sand,
the calm at the edges,
the fisherman down at the dock.

Plaintive mourning doves
sound like morning and evening
        (the same)
even 600 miles away.

My name in the sand
is unfinished without yours.

We are all just the daughters
of the boys who joined the military branch
that took them away to the water,
only to come back and raise
us on this breathing, shallow
prairie.

Haircuts on the Back Porch

My father, sensing
my need to do something he cannot,
asks me for a haircut.
This is one thing I can do well for him.
His head is an atlas
of white rivers,
all scars from so many days
spent on his back,
looking up into the gaping mouth
of the steel-toothed combine.
Eyes small without glasses,
I cannot tell if he looks more
like his mother or his father.
I brush the last of the graying hairs
off his bare shoulders, slack with muscle.
The swallows will come soon to
spear the tufts for their nests.

How a Midwest Farm Girl Tells You She Loves You

Had my ancestors believed in trees,
I would carve:
initials, arrows piercing
hearts, 4-evers
into every thick silver maple
shooting up from the prairie.
Had my ancestors stopped and settled
5 hours north, we would be in Canada right now
and I would spell out our love in ketchup chips.
Had my ancestors turned up money instead of clay and sod,
I would buy you a big house with a wraparound porch.

Since we are here,
now,
this is how I declare my love:
We believe in wind.
So, I take you for a walk to the Missouri river so
the banks buffer the gusts and you have
to lean in close to hear me.
We believe in the two-step.
So, I dance close with you, my hand
splayed low on your back.
We believe in denim.
So, follow my eyes down the lines of your swaying hips.

Together, we will pour our love into Happy Hour, into clover,
into antelope and potlucks, into red beers with green olives, into
porches and the fiddle and, finally, into
the smack dab center
of our big, Midwestern hearts.

Leather Stretcher

My father tells me to get my work boots
shakily balanced out on the top
rail of our deck so the farm mutt won't
drag them down to the crick.
The Wal-Mart boots
aren't made for the Badlands.

I come home from trail work each evening,
limping and favoring my raw, rubbed heels.
Mornings, I have to brace myself for the weight
of my sun-burnt body on my swollen insteps.
I can't put a clamp on the hurt.

I lay the boots at his feet and wait.
His large, browned hands hold
a leather stretcher made from cast iron.
It was his father's and has to be at least
eighty years old.

I watch his unlined face,
the furrow of his eyebrows.
Same as mine, peaked like we're
never happy, and my mom always says
we both frown with just those.
Hazel eyes, again mine.
The man's a perfectionist, and I
know he's lonely at the top.

When he asks how my day was,
I say, *Good. I got caught up on a slippery*
switchback and almost lost my thumb when my
Pulaski slammed down on my hand. I show
him the flat bruise. He says, *A Ukrainian hurt*
by a Polish tool.

I press my forearm to his, mine
dwarfed there in size. *Look, I'm getting*
almost as dark as you. Though he is still
three shades darker then the tannest
part of me: the back of my neck.

He asks where I hurt. Not brave
enough to really say, I point to the boots' make-believe
skin and tendons. We don't say directions
in right or left. We say east or west.
The southeast side of the arch? He asks.
I nod. The tool hovers there and goes to work.

Paraska in Spring

This Homestead Act of 1862, giving her husband land
like the land back in the Old Country.

This land was good.
Good for wheat and barley.
Good for chickens and potatoes.
Good for Our Lord Jesus Christ and baptism.
Good for a woman whose back proves to be strong enough.

A winter of deep freeze. An alcoholic husband
who beat his cold hands into the land, into the cattle, into her.
It was all white, then brown. Dead things clung to
the horizon. She buried a son.
And then, blessedly, the first break of spring sun
over the hilly tundra. Her world
thawed; the crocuses, dense and purple,
seeped through the melting snow, and she was

standing alone

in her sod kitchen,
watching Dakota bloom golden.

In five years, she would hate how river bottoms
dried up into cracked heels.
She buried her
third child and her heart split in two.
In fifteen years, she would be buried with
St. Demetrius, her back broken by the alcoholic.
Her headstone picture would be
pretty and young, like when she first crossed this prairie
clutching a piece
of flowered embroidery around her narrow shoulders.

But then, oh then, that first Spring?

When she walked outside for that first
time with bare forearms, carrying a chipped
pitcher to hold water pumped
from the well,
and she breathed in, deep, the smell
of sweet grass, of loosening earth,
she must have felt like
the tight fist of peony, ready to open into life.

Her Sunday

My mother's hands: square and pink,
hands that have gripped the scaly, yellowed legs
of headless chickens as they were bucked
by the plucking wheel during the chilly ashen mornings
we butchered. They are not piano-playing hands,
but when she sits down at her dark, wooden piano
that took the strength of my dad and
all my uncles to jostle through the front door,
her hands begin to spin out something transcendent—
maybe it's *Hymn by Vangelis.*
Those short fingers and able palms,
so hilly and freckled they could have been the shoulders
of a swimmer, harvest the lithe notes
buried deep within the innards of the instrument
—and from my basement bedroom—
I hear her and cry.

Under the flat stare of Ukrainian saints,
she sways and plays her music.
Those same hands unload trucks of wheat in August
and are pecked by jealous hens as she reaches for their eggs.
I sometimes envision I am the giddy bride
walking out to *Wedding March*, or I am the groom
whose back straightens at the opening note of *Canon in D.*
For now, though, I stand as a sentry behind her, keeping
a ready eye on her kind face.
Waiting for the nod of her head
to turn the page, I swell with pride that I
am the one she always chooses.

I am protective of my mother's hands;
they have cupped my smudged face
since I slept in the crook of her arm.
Lately, they trace the clean lines
around my lips and eyes while we
both wonder where years have gone.

Her hands, their quilted heaviness,
warm on my neck.

In Case I Croak

Every Thanksgiving, he herds
us outside. In the bright scarceness,
he faces us.
"In case I croak," he says,
here's where you shut off the water.
Here's where I keep the combination to the safe.
Here's the titles to the pickups."
Each fall, when all us kids are home for a long weekend, we go
over what do in case my father dies.

We are all grown now.
We are not the children who used to flinch
at his footsteps or beg him to hit us flyballs.
Inside the house, we all crowd around the fuse
box in the utility room as he points one blood-
blistered finger towards the dishwasher fuse,
the fridge fuse.
"In case I croak," he says.
We trudge downstairs to his old
roll-top desk,
where this man has kept a record of
everything he has done, bought, fixed, and built
in the past fifty years.
Block writing in blue ink on thin, lined paper.

He has taken to wearing Hawaiian shirts
and completely shaves his bald head and is slowly
turning into the father I have been waiting for.

In case you croak, I think,
I won't be worrying about the pipes freezing.
I'll forget to check my oil and the combination
to the safe, and even, to open up the chicken coop.
No, in case you croak, I'll
take a walk down by the crick to
look for wild asparagus.
If I find a patch, I will pick it, take it to the
home you used to call a glorified trailer house,
and cook it
steamed with a little cream and almonds,
just the way you liked it.
And in early Spring, I'll gather my brother
and sister from our corners of Dakota
and we'll walk North for a mile
to see if the crocuses have bloomed.
In case you croak, Dad,
we'll search for purple dotting the brown
prairie.

Rowboat

When I press my forearms to my nose,
I smell softly scorched wood.
The smell that comes from
curving over a table saw all day,
cleanly slicing fresh two-by-fours.
My German from Russia grandma,
who always smelled like Merits and Avon lipstick,
told me to give them all something.
I give them sawdust.
A dry fragrance, flammable and unswept.
A lady in the English Department stopped short
in front of me today, inhaled deeply and told
me I smelled wonderful.
Her father must have been a carpenter,
and there I stood, that solidly human
link between memory and the nose that
scientists won a Nobel for not long ago.
Wood chips cling to my hair,
tucked in deep to the sink of my ear.
When I take my shirt off, I look in the mirror
and see some hybrid between a girl and a pheasant,
a neck ringed with dirt and sunburn.
My jeans are caked with the old, iridescent
gas that won't seep into the floor
of my dad's shop.
I leave them in a sculpted pile near the
doorway so as not to get any grease
on the carpet or Lazyboy.
My shoulders aren't broad enough yet,
but will be like knotty pine soon.
Calluses, a Killdeer Mountain ridge
edging my palms, are perennial.

When men shake my hand they will think,
Wow, this girl's a worker.
Maybe they'll do a double take at
my clumsy knuckles and wonder
if I'm a girl at all.
Maybe I'm one of those they saw
on the Discovery Channel late last night
whose parents raised them the wrong gender.
Maybe underneath it all, those men
will ache to know what I am hiding.
See me out on the Big Water,
sculling past in a cedar rowboat
I built,
sanded, scaled
leveled, finished.
Tire-soled sandals wedged against the
steamed, bowed sides.
A banner of sun-bleached hair and
stumble upon the faint smell of
forest fire I leave in my wake.

Lindy Obach was raised on a grain farm on the edge of the badlands of western North Dakota and currently teaches writing and literature for The University of South Dakota at University Center in Sioux Falls. She loves working with her immigrant, military, and other non-traditional students. Lindy's poetry has been published in *The South Dakota Review, Midwestern Gothic, The Blue Bear Review, Scurfpea Press, The Ukrainian Cultural Institute*, and more. She has been a teacher-consultant with the Dakota Writing Project since 2007 and enjoys flea markets, old pickups, and biking along the Big Sioux River. As a poet, Lindy is most interested in notions of home, love, identity, and the Dakota prairie.

www.ingramcontent.com/pod-product-compliance
Lightning Source LLC
LaVergne TN
LVHW090015090426
835509LV00035BA/1269